Children of the World

New Zealand

For their help in the preparation of *Children of the World: New Zealand,* the editors gratefully thank Kathleen and David Reed of the University of Wisconsin-Milwaukee; Thayer Reed, Milwaukee, Wis,; David Rendel of Mallinson Rendel Publishers Ltd., Wellington, New Zealand; and the Embassy of New Zealand, Washington, D.C.

Library of Congress Cataloging-in-Publication Data

Yanagi, Akinobu, 1951-
  New Zealand.

  (Children of the world)
  Based on the original Japanese work by Akinobu Yanagi.
  Summary: Presents the life of a ten-year-old boy on
a New Zealand sheep ranch describing his family, home,
school, and amusements and some of the traditions and
celebrations of his country.
  1. New Zealand — Juvenile literature. 2. Children —
New Zealand — Juvenile literature. [1. New Zealand —
Social life and customs. 2. Family life — New Zealand]
I. Knowlton, MaryLee, 1946-   . II. Sachner,
Mark, 1948-   . III. Title. IV. Series: Children
of the world (Milwaukee, Wis.)
DU408.Y36 1987   993.1   86-42801
ISBN 1-55532-187-9
ISBN 1-55532-162-3 (lib. bdg.)   JUL 2 3 1987

North American edition first published in 1987 by

Gareth Stevens, Inc.
7221 West Green Tree Road   Milwaukee, Wisconsin 53223, USA

This work was originally published in shortened form consisting of section I only.
Photographs and original text copyright © 1986 by Akinobu Yanagi.
Photograph on page 52 courtesy of New Zealand Department of Maori Affairs.
First and originally published by Kaisei-sha Publishing Co., Ltd., Tokyo.
World English rights arranged with Kaisei-sha Publishing Co., Ltd. through
Japan Foreign-Rights Centre.

Typeset by Ries Graphics ltd., Milwaukee.
Design: Laurie Shock.
Map design: Gary Moseley.

1 2 3 4 5 6 7 8 9 92 91 90 89 88 87

Children of the World

New Zealand

Photography by
Akinobu Yanagi

Edited by
MaryLee Knowlton &
Mark J. Sachner

Gareth Stevens Publishing
Milwaukee

... a note about *Children of the World:*

The children of the world live in fishing towns and urban centers, on islands and in mountain valleys, on sheep ranches and fruit farms. This series follows one child in each country through the pattern of his or her life. Candid photographs show the children with their families, at school, at play, and in their communities. The text describes the dreams of the children and, often through their own words, tells how they see themselves and their lives.

Each book also explores events that are unique to the country in which the child lives, including festivals, religious ceremonies, and national holidays. The *Children of the World* series does more than tell about foreign countries. It introduces the children of each country and shows readers what it is like to be a child in that country.

... and about *New Zealand:*

Hamish McLachlan lives in a village that is 180 miles square (466 sq. km) but has only 60 houses. All the villagers run sheep stations, and Hamish is already a worker on his parents' station even though he is only ten years old. It is said that you may go for days in New Zealand without seeing another person, but there's never a day without sheep in this land of three million people and sixty million sheep.

To enhance this book's value in libraries and classrooms, comprehensive reference sections include up-to-date data about New Zealand's geography, demographics, language, currency, education, culture, industry, and natural resources. *New Zealand* also features a bibliography, research topics, activity projects, and discussions of such subjects as Wellington, the country's history, political system, ethnic and religious composition, and language.

The living conditions and experiences of children in New Zealand vary tremendously according to economic, environmental, and ethnic circumstances. The reference sections help bring to life for young readers the diversity and richness of the culture and heritage of New Zealand. Of particular interest are discussions of the Maori, the native culture that has so emphatically made its presence felt in the language and tradition of New Zealand.

CONTENTS

I hope you learn about New Zealand
Hamish Stuart McLachlan

LIVING IN NEW ZEALAND:
Hamish, a Young Rancher

Hamish McLachlan is ten. He lives in New Zealand, a country about the size of Colorado. The human population is about three million. But the sheep population is 60 million. They say there may be days when you don't see any people. But there is never a day without sheep.

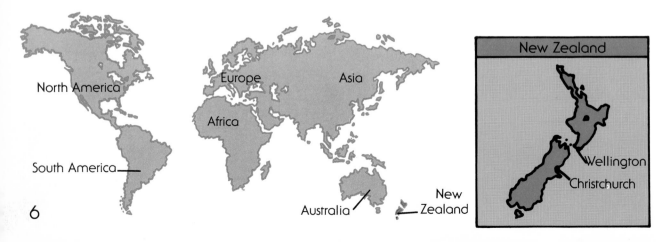

North America

South America

Europe

Africa

Asia

Australia

New Zealand

New Zealand

Wellington

Christchurch

A quarter mile-long (.4 km) dirt road connects Hamish's house to the main highway, National Rt. 1.

A view of Omihi from a hill.

Vaccinating sheep against disease.

The sheared wool is gathered
and ranked into three grades.

The sheep minus their woolly coats.

Hamish rounds up sheep. After shearing, he counts them and sweeps up after them.

Sheep Farming

The McLachlans have 2,000 sheep and 300 head of cattle. Their ranch is an average size family station. It has 375 acres (152 hectares) of meadows.

Sheep shearing takes place in August, at the end of New Zealand's winter. This is the busiest time of the year. Professional shearers, called *rousterers,* come and shear sheep. They work from early morning till late at night. One rousterer can shear 200 sheep a day. Hamish is very busy, too. He counts the sheep sheared and sweeps around them.

The lambing season is August and September. Many young sheep are giving birth to their first lambs. These sheep are gathered in a corral, or paddock. Hamish's father checks them twice a day. Sometimes a sheep cannot push its baby out of its body, or a lamb has trouble coming out of its mother. In these cases, Hamish's father pulls the lambs out.

Lambs are raised on their mother's milk for several months. Then they begin to feed themselves. Each mother can raise only one lamb at a time, however. Twin or lost lambs must be taken into the house and fed milk every day. Hamish and his sister, Philisty, must take care of these lambs.

Lambs are very cute. When they get hungry, they call for milk and walk around the children's legs. Watching the lambs eat and grow, the children feel like mother sheep themselves. At the end of January the lambs are sold. This year the family sold 1100 lambs.

Some lambs are lost or twin lambs. These lambs cannot be fed by their mothers.
Hamish and his sister, Philisty, must care for them.

13

A lamb can walk by itself 30-40 minutes after it is born.

Hamish and Philisty play on the bales of hay.

In summer, the farm work is not as demanding as in winter. However, the McLachlans must prepare food for winter and for dry spells. They use a machine to roll the hay and place it in rows. This year they prepared eighty 500-pound (227-kg) bales. Hamish loves the smell of fresh hay.

Hamish driving a truck over the large meadow.

Using a movable fence.

Taking a break with a favorite pet.

Driving sheep by clapping hands and shouting.

16

Today the weather looks threatening. It has been windy since morning, and now it looks like rain. Hamish and his father must hurry with their work. They must herd the sheep quickly into the barn. They drive the sheep by shouting and clapping. This usually gets the sheep moving. Today, however, the sheep do not seem to be in any hurry. Hamish wishes his family had a sheep dog.

Hamish plans to have his own sheep station some day. When he does, he will also have sheep dogs. Then he can drive sheep by simply whistling to the dogs.

Hamish's father and mother let him drive the family truck. He doesn't have a driver's license, of course, so he cannot drive on public roads. His parents let him drive only in the meadow, where there is nothing to hit. In New Zealand, young people can get driver's licenses when they are fifteen.

Black Angus.

Cattle Farming

The McLachlans raise Black Angus cattle for beef. Today they move 120 head of cattle 4½ miles (7¼ km). The cattle are going from one paddock to another near the mountains. Hamish rides his bicycle. His father and older brother play catch with a rugby ball. This is the way they drive cattle! Two hours later, they reach the mountain paddock.

The herd moves slowly on National Rt. 1.

Separating male and female cattle.

Hamish's mother and sister arrive by truck with lunch.

The McLachlan house.
The clothes-drying stand twirls like a windmill in the wind.

At Home with Hamish and His Family

Hamish's house is six years old. His mother planned it with many of the features she has seen in the U.S. and Europe. Triple wooden boards keep it cool in the summer and warm in winter. It has five bedrooms, a living room, a kitchen, a dining room, and a laundry room. Like many New Zealand homes, it has a clothes-drying stand. If it rains, the clothes are left out till they dry again.

20

National Rt. 1 runs past Hamish's house.
Many long-distance trucks pass by.
Many are loaded with sheared wool.

Behind the house, a train runs twice a day
carrying passengers and freight.

A mail box. On it are the names of the farm and family.
The small red flag is a sign for both the letter carrier and
the family. It tells the carrier that there is mail to be
picked up. It tells the family that mail has been delivered.

A rare treat: The entire family dines together.

The McLachlan family has five members: Hamish; his brother, Sandy; his sister, Philisty; and his mother and father, Julia and Bruce. Sandy is sixteen. He goes to boarding school in Christchurch. Philisty is five. She attends Omihi Primary School with Hamish.

The staple food is meat and potatoes and other vegetables. The family usually eats in the kitchen. Tonight, the whole family is together, so they eat in the dining room to celebrate.

Hamish and his family usually eat all three meals at the kitchen table.

Dinner conversation usually concerns the station and sports. Sometimes they talk about the children's plans for the future. Hamish wants to run a sheep station. He plans to study agriculture at Canterbury University after high school.

The whole family enjoys sports. Sandy likes rugby and boating. Their mother is good at long-distance running. Their father has played rugby since he was young. Everybody wonders what Philisty will take up.

Hamish helps his mother and sneaks a taste of powdered milk.

Tonight's dessert: Ice cream, peaches, and whipped cream.

Watching slides of Japan.

After dinner, Hamish and Philisty sometimes watch TV or play games.

Working and Relaxing

After dinner, the whole family works together. Everyone clears the table and washes dishes. Hamish does what he has to. But he prefers outdoor work to house work.

After the dishes are done, the family relaxes in the living room. Hamish and his mother both love to read. His mother has shown him the books she read as a young girl. They are about the settling of New Zealand. He especially likes books about young people growing up on North American farms. He also likes books about pioneer life in Canada and the United States.

This evening, they enjoy looking at slides of Japan. Hamish's father took them when he visited Japan on an agricultural study trip. Whenever he can, he studies modern ways of improving herds and production. Wool and beef are the major products of the sheep and cattle stations. These products are New Zealand's major exports. Therefore, they are very important to the economy.

Hamish's desk.

Hamish's Room

Some of Hamish's favorite books.

Hamish enjoys studying math.

Hamish enjoys reading before going to bed.

All of the McLachlan children have their own rooms. Last spring Hamish got a large desk from his father. Although it looks new, the desk belonged to his father for 30 years. It was used for keeping herd records.

Hamish usually goes to bed around nine o'clock. He likes to read till he falls asleep. Now he's reading a book about a pilot in the New Zealand armed forces.

Going into Christchurch

Christchurch is the biggest city in the South Island. It has a population of 320,000. This makes it the third biggest city in New Zealand. It is 40 miles (64 km) south of Hamish's home, and he goes there with his family several times a month. There are no post offices, banks, or stores in the village of Omihi, so they usually have a lot to do when they go. In fact, they have so much planned that they must keep a list of things to do. Today Hamish goes with his father and his sister, Philisty.

Christchurch is often called the "Garden City" because its British planners left plenty of space for parks and gardens. Throughout the city, and especially along the River Avon, flower gardens bloom. These gardens remind many visitors of Honolulu.

Hamish, Philisty, and their father stroll through a downtown square in Christchurch.

Christchurch has many activities for Hamish and his family. Just strolling and looking at the many shops can fill an afternoon with fun. One attraction for all are the many restaurants. Hamish's favorite is a place where he can eat fried chicken.

In Christchurch, markets line the National Highway.
This one sells mostly vegetables.

A meat shop.

Visiting the wool factory.

The River Avon runs right through Christchurch.

After shopping for food, the children and their father go to the wool factory. The sheared wool from sheep all over the island is gathered here and graded by quality.

Often when they are in town, they go to the Botanic Gardens or to the Canterbury Museum. Hamish likes the section of the museum that tells and shows the early history of New Zealand. He is especially interested in learning about New Zealand's earliest settlers, the Maori. He also wants to learn about one of the animals the Maori hunted, the Moa bird. The Moa is now extinct.

The River Avon winds through the center of the city. It is so clean that trout live there even now. Only children under 12 can fish there. Hamish's brother Sandy belongs to his school's boat club and practices on the river.

Hamish's sister Philisty has a favorite place to go in Christchurch. It is the Aquarium Zoo. Here children and adults can watch lighted windows filled with many colorful sea animals.

A view of Christchurch.

Mr. Brown, Hamish's teacher, makes the rounds among the students in class.

Hamish and His Friends at School

Hamish's school is the Omihi Primary School. It has three teachers and forty-three pupils from five to thirteen years old. In New Zealand, children start school on their fifth birthday. When they first enter school, children learn the national anthem in their first music class. Every Wednesday morning at Hamish's school, everyone assembles to sing the anthem and do folk dances.

33

Hamish's school has two classrooms, a library, a meeting hall, a swimming pool, and a sports field. Classes run from nine o'clock in the morning to three in the afternoon, Monday through Friday.

The students have no homework and leave all their books and notebooks in their desks when they go home. Mr. Brown, Hamish's teacher, thinks it is enough for them to study in class. He also thinks children should play and help with chores at home. Hamish has a six-week summer vacation, a two-week winter vacation, and a two-week break in May to help with farm work.

Hamish pays careful attention to class discussion.

Children in the upper grades ring the bell to start and end each class period.

The library.

Lessons from English class.

up study.

Inside the desks!

In the morning, Hamish studies English and math. Math is his favorite subject, and he is at the top of his class. In the afternoon he has classes in science, social studies, physical education, and music. Children from five to thirteen are in Hamish's class. To study certain subjects, they are divided into four groups.

When the noon bell rings, the children dash for their lunch boxes. When the weather is good, they have their sandwiches, cookies, fruit, and drinks outside.

Lunch time. Girls and boys eat separately.

A folk dance. The school hall is also used for village meetings. ↗   ↙The school yard.

Hamish's school and classmates: 43 students, ages 5-13.

Playing in the school yard.

The school bus.

School's Out!

After school, Hamish often gets off the bus at his aunt's house. She keeps three horses, and Hamish is learning to ride. He cannot go very fast now, but he hopes soon to be able to gallop freely through the fields.

40

Hamish learns to ride at his aunt's farm.

Hamish's hiding place is in these trees.

Woodland plants near Hamish's home.

Hamish's Hiding Place

Hamish has a hiding place in a large tree near his house. His brother built it and handed it down to him. Children in New Zealand often build this kind of place for themselves. They call it a *climbing frame.*

43

A soccer game.

Sports

New Zealanders love to play and watch sports. Two players on the All Blacks, the best rugby team in the world, they say, come from Omihi, so the villagers are wild about rugby. On weekends, adults play rugby on a lighted field till late at night.

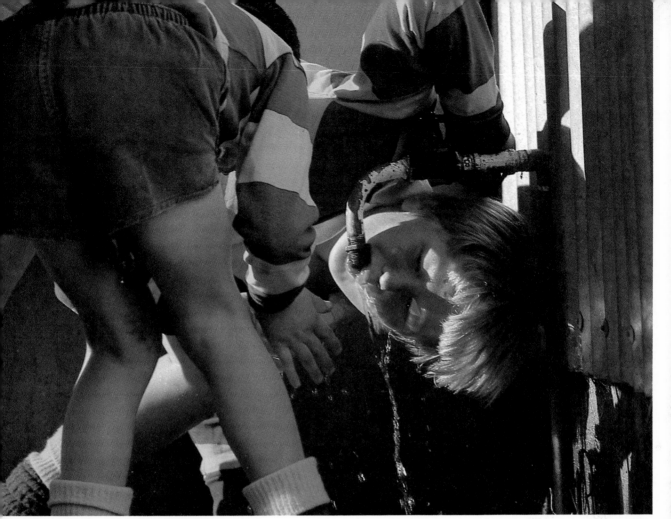

Hamish and his teammates played hard.
His team finished fourth out of six in the meet, but he enjoys working up a sweat.

Today is the yearly district sports meet. Six schools have come to compete. Boys play rugby and soccer. Girls play softball and *net ball,* a sport like basketball. Hamish plays on his school's soccer team. Working on a sheep station takes lots of strength, and Hamish sees sports as a way of building up his body.

FOR YOUR INFORMATION: New Zealand

Official name: The Dominion of New Zealand

Capital: Wellington

History

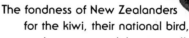

The fondness of New Zealanders for the kiwi, their national bird, has prompted them to call themselves *kiwis*.

The Maori

Legend says that in 1350 A.D., seven boats arrived in New Zealand. They were filled with Maori settlers from the Polynesian Islands. These boats were known as the "Great Fleet". Archaeologists have found evidence that Polynesians began settling New Zealand much earlier than 1350, between 950 and 1000 A.D. The Great Fleet, however, is thought of as the beginning of modern Maori history.

The Maori settlers called the new country *Aotearoa*. This means "land of the long, white cloud." Each boatload formed one community, or *pa*. Each village had a *tohunga,* or tribal elder. The tohunga kept the genealogy, or family history, of every tribe member in his head. He told and retold these histories in songs.

The Maori were expert fishermen and bird snarers. They planted fruits and vegetables and ate fish, small animals, and game birds. Winter in New Zealand was the first Maori exposure to cold. Before coming to Aotearoa, they had worn clothing made of soft bark called *tapa* cloth. Now they were faced with a harsher climate. The women learned to weave and braid flax into warmer clothing.

The Maori had a highly developed society. They enjoyed the arts of debate and warfare. Their society worked on a system called *tapu*. Tapu was a series of taboos, or prohibitions. One violation of tapu might be trespassing on a grave. Or it might be showing disrespect for parts of the body. Such violations would cause Maori gods to take away their support from the violator. This would leave the violator unprotected.

Family life was central to the society. Children have always been cared for by their grandparents. This leaves parents free to work. The Maori adore children, and orphans are joyfully welcomed into new homes. In Maori society, no child should ever be unprotected.

The bodies of men of honor were highly decorated. Tattoos covered their faces, thighs, and buttocks with swirls and spirals. Women had more modest tattoos, usually just on the lips and chin.

The Dutch and French

In 1642 Dutch explorers found the islands, but the Maori drove them out. Dutch interest in the region was very brief. Dutch explorer Abel Tasman first named it

Staten Landt. Later Dutch geographers renamed it *Nieuw Zeeland.* In the late 1700s and early 1800s, French explorers also showed an interest in New Zealand. The Maori drove them out, too.

The British

In 1769, Captain James Cook arrived in New Zealand. He explored the islands three times and made a limited peace between the Maori and Britain. Not until 1840 was a more formal treaty between the Maori and the British agreed on. At the time of Cook's visits there were about 200,000 Maoris living in New Zealand. In 1814 the first Christian missionaries settled. They came up with an alphabet for the Maori language. Until that time, Maori had not been a written language. The missionaries also taught the Maori English and Christianity. They introduced the Maori to flower gardens, sheep, cattle, gunpowder, and diseases.

The Maori and the Pakeha

The British had a big effect on Maori culture. The flower gardens are everywhere now in New Zealand, and sheep and cattle are vital to the economy. Not everything the British brought to the Maori was helpful, however. The British introduced rabbits. As a result, the vegetation that provided a balance of nature was, for a time, largely destroyed. British gunpowder caused more violence among Maori tribes. Most of all, their diseases killed thousands of Maori. By 1900, only about 40,000 Maoris remained. Today, the Maori population has grown once again to about 200,000, what it was before the arrival of the *pakeha*, or foreigner.

Independence from Britain

On February 6, 1840, the Treaty of Waitangi was signed between the British and the Maori. On that day, New Zealand became a British colony. Queen Victoria was its ruler. The Maori were given land guarantees. They were also made full citizens. Even so, land disputes resulted in violence for many years after. In the 1860s and 1870s, land wars between Maori and Pakeha resulted in the loss of Maori lives, land, and *mana*. Mana is a word for Maori pride and honor.

Today the Maori are still trying to reclaim land taken from them. The courts have often ruled in their favor. Some New Zealanders, including many Maori, see the Treaty of Waitangi as the start of a long struggle for Maori justice.

In 1853, Britain gave New Zealand the right of self-government. And in 1907 it became an independent country and a member of the British Commonwealth.

New Zealand Today

After World War II New Zealand, Australia, and the United States signed the ANZUS Treaty. They promised to help defend each other. In the 1980s, however, New Zealand developed a peace policy which rejects nuclear arms. This means that New Zealand will not let nuclear-armed foreign ships into its ports. The government of the 49

United States has made its displeasure known to New Zealand. In 1986, the U.S. withdrew its commitment to offer New Zealand military help.

In 1985, French spies sunk the 160-foot (50 m) *Rainbow Warrior* in a New Zealand harbor. The boat was preparing to lead other Greenpeace boats in a protest against French nuclear testing. A photographer was killed. Afterwards, the French government tried to cover up its role in the bombing. Both the bombing and the cover-up outraged the New Zealand government and people opposed to nuclear warfare throughout the world.

Most of the French spies escaped. New Zealand officials arrested two, however. They were tried and convicted of manslaughter. In response to their agents' imprisonment, France blocked New Zealand's exports to France. In 1986, the United Nations arranged a settlement. In this settlement, France agreed to pay seven million dollars to New Zealand. France also agreed to stop blocking sales of New Zealand butter and meat to Europe. New Zealand agreed to release the two secret agents to serve the rest of their sentence in French custody.

Here is what one New Zealander said about his country's feelings about nuclear arms: "A lot of people here believe nuclear arms should have no role in our defense — or in solving world problems."

Population and Ethnic Groups

The population of New Zealand is about 3,500,000. With between 800,000 and 900,000 people, Auckland is the largest city. Wellington and Christchurch, each with between 300,000 and 350,000 people, are the next largest. About 56% of New Zealand's total population live in Auckland, Wellington, Christchurch, Dunedin, and Hamilton. About 90% of the population is of European descent, mostly British. About 10% is Polynesian. Today Auckland is the world's largest Polynesian city.

The Polynesian population is primarily Maori, and it is descended from the original inhabitants of the country. The Maori presence is strongly felt in New Zealand. Unlike that of the North American Indian, however, the presence is not of a conquered and deprived minority. The Maoris of today are a group of proud participants in the continuing culture. How come?

Perhaps the reason is that New Zealand was colonized later than North America. Or perhaps it is that Christian missionaries intervened in favor of the Maori to limit their abuse. The Maori had many conflicts with the European settlers. But despite these conflicts, the Maori received much more humane treatment than did native Americans. The Maori were immediately made full citizens. Also, their land was protected and developed as part of the country's assets. The Maori have used the courts to ensure their land rights. The culture they had established has lived on. And it has lived on as a familiar part of the total culture, not just as an isolated curiosity. The Maori term *tatou-tatou* - "us-us" - represents the goal of Maori and Pakeha unity.

In 1945, only 15% of the Maori lived in the cities. Today over 70% are city dwellers, mostly in the North Island. For many of these Maoris, this change has resulted in economic, educational, and social problems. Programs exist to provide educational aid, legal assistance, vocational training, and welfare services. Young Maori are struggling to find an identity that is different from that of their elders but within the idea of *Maoritanga*. Maoritanga means the Maori way of doing things.

The Maoritanga movement has three main beliefs: 1. Maori identity is important to Maori people. 2. Maori culture is part of New Zealand's national identity. This therefore means that Maori culture is important to New Zealand as a whole. 3. Problems exist and they need attention.

The Maori tradition is made up of a few simple attitudes that control their beliefs and actions. Maori people are loyal to their extended family. This includes the mother, father, sisters, brothers, grandparents, and often cousins, nieces, and nephews. Besides their own family, they express *aroha*, or love and understanding, for others. They show hospitality to all visitors.

Language

Most people speak English, the national language. A New Zealand variety of English has developed as well. In fact, there are many words and expressions peculiar to New Zealand that North Americans would not understand. The Maori language is also a language of New Zealand. For many years, the number of Maori speakers had declined. But today, that number is getting larger. Many place names come from the Maori. The Maori language has five vowels, eight consonants, and one combination sound.

These are the vowels:
a as in *father* or *cut*
e as in *lend*
i as in *green*
o as in *order*
u as in *moon*

These are the consonants:
h k m n p r t w

This is the combined sound: *ng* as in *singer*

No other consonants come together except *wh*, as in *where*. Every syllable ends in a vowel. No vowels are accented more strongly than others. When two vowels come together, each is pronounced separately. Therefore, *Aotearoa*, the Maori name for *New Zealand*, is pronounced as follows: ah-oh-teh-ah-roh-ah.

Religion

Christianity is not the only religion in New Zealand, but it dominates. The main denominations are Anglican (Episcopal), Presbyterian, Roman Catholic, and Methodist.

Some Maori children learn both English and Maori at a young age.

Education

Children from six to fifteen years old must go to school. Most children enter a primary school on their fifth birthday. Girls and boys mostly go to different schools. Even in the public schools, most students wear uniforms. School is not required after children turn 15. Still, more than half of the pupils continue to the upper grades. University education is free to everyone. Students must pass entrance exams to qualify.

Children in New Zealand have a six-week summer vacation. Their vacation starts after Christmas. They also have several shorter vacations throughout the school year.

Some areas of New Zealand are very remote or underpopulated. These areas may not be able to support a school. The State Correspondence School is a big part of the educational system for children in these areas. Children are sent their lessons, which they complete and return for grading. Daily classes are given over the radio. Students take exams at the end of the school year. From time to time, teachers visit children in their homes. Several times a year, students attend "school week" gatherings. At school week, they get to work with other children. The students of the correspondence school have their own school magazine and club activities.

Classes for all children in New Zealand are arranged according to a national program. All children must study oral and written language. This includes reading and handwriting. They must also study math, social studies, science, arts and crafts, and music. Finally, they must take physical education — swimming and outdoor recreation. Some schools offer courses in the Maori language. Some schools have many Maori and Pacific Island children. At these schools, English language programs are offered for the younger children who may not speak English at home.

Art and Music

The Maori give New Zealand its truly unique artistic flavor. The Maori made up songs for many occasions. Maori music was different from western music in several ways. For one thing, their melodies had a more limited scale than western music. Often the songs had four part harmonies, with the fourth part for the children. Often Maori singers accompanied their music with face and body movements. Their instruments included trumpets made of shells and wood, nose flutes, drums, and gongs.

A song called the "Hawaiian Farewell" begins, "Now is the hour when we must say good-bye." This song is familiar to many North American children. Yet most do not know that this is an ancient Maori song.

According to Maori religious beliefs, artists must not compete with the divine creator. This means that artists could not show life as the divine creator made it. For that reason, traditional Maori art was not realistic, or life-like. Rather, it showed distorted images of humans and animals. The Maoris were highly skilled woodworkers. They decorated war canoes, ornaments, weapons, and utensils. Even today a Maori *whare*, or house, is often beautifully carved in traditional designs.

The art and artifacts of the Maori are regarded as treasures. Therefore, they are guarded by the tribal elders. They are not for sale and, until 1984, had not been allowed out of the country. In 1984, the Metropolitan Museum of Art in New York had a major exhibit of New Zealand's Maori art. In keeping with tradition, the tribal elders accompanied the exhibit to New York.

Today New Zealand craftspeople work in clay and textiles. Their pottery and cloth mirror the color and feel of the natural world. The colors are rich and earth-toned.

Sports

New Zealanders are very sports-minded. Children are taught to swim as soon as they start kindergarten, and sports in general play a big part in the school program.

The national sport is rugby, and the national team, the All Blacks, is world famous. The All Blacks play teams from Australia, France, England, and South Africa. In recent years, games against South Africa have been the scene of large protests. At these games, some people have expressed their disapproval of apartheid. Apartheid is a policy of South Africa's white government. It denies rights and freedom to black people. Many people in New Zealand do not want their team to play the South African team.

Rugby is much like the North American game of football. Players score by kicking the ball between the goal posts or by touching the ball to the ground over the goal line. Unlike football, though, players do not wear heavy padding. As in soccer, play only stops when the ball goes out of bounds or when someone scores or commits a foul. The game thus seems quite fast-paced to people used to the many pauses in football games. Each team has 15 players who can all kick, carry, and score.

In addition to rugby, some New Zealanders like cricket, softball, horseracing, and boating. Many New Zealanders love backpacking and hiking, which they call *tramping*. Mountain climbing, too, has a long tradition in New Zealand. In 1953, a team of explorers became the first to reach the top of Mt. Everest, the world's highest mountain. This team included a New Zealander, Sir Edmund Hillary.

A college rugby match in Christchurch.

Climate

New Zealand has a variety of climates, from the subtropical climate of the north to the almost subarctic climate of the southern mountains. As a whole, though, the climate is moderate, without extremes of hot or cold. New Zealand is a sunny country, with about six hours of sunshine a day. The average yearly rainfall is 25-60 inches (0.6-1.5 m), and rain comes in brief, heavy downpours. Because New Zealand is below the equator, its seasons are the opposite of North America's. The summer months are November, December, and January.

Land

New Zealand is about halfway between the equator and the South Pole. It consists of two main islands — the North Island and the South Island. It is about 1100 miles (1770 km) from the farthest southern point of the South Island to the most northern tip of the North Island. A third and much smaller island — Stewart Island — lies to the south of them. The total land area is about 104,000 square miles (270,000 sq. km). Three-quarters of this area is more than 660 ft (200 m) above sea level. Australia is 930 miles (1496 km) to the northwest.

The South Island has plains suitable for crops and grazing. And because it is so close to Antarctica, the South Island has glaciers and beautiful mountain lakes. The North Island has rich meadows and vast forests. The thick forests are safe for hikers, because New Zealand has no snakes, poisonous insects, or deadly animals. In fact, till the Maori came in 1350 bringing with them a rat and a dog, New Zealand had no mammals at all! When the missionaries came in 1814, they brought sheep and cattle. They also brought rabbits, which caused trouble as their population boomed.

The North Island has three volcanoes. Two are active: Ruapehu, 9184 ft (2800 m), and Ngauruhoe, 7515 ft (2290 m). Tongariro, 6460 ft (1970 m), is dormant.

More than 70% of New Zealanders live in the North Island. Here the climate is milder, and industry is more developed. Despite the industrial development, however, New Zealand is not like other, more densely populated countries. New Zealand is free from many of the pollution problems that affect these countries. Citizen and government groups guard their land, air, and water resources carefully.

New Zealanders live with the threat of earthquakes. In this way, they are much like people in California. It is customary not to hang pictures with glass over a bed. Many buildings are specially designed to withstand shifts in the earth's surface. Children take part in earthquake drills in their classrooms.

Natural Resources

New Zealand's main natural resource is timber. In 1886. Mt. Tarawera, in the North Island, erupted, spreading volcanic ash over a large part of the island. It buried local villages and spread dust for over 20 miles (32 km). In the 1920's the country began a program of tree planting, importing the California Pinus radiata. This tree produces a soft wood that is well suited to the soil left by the volcano. The success of the timber industry has led to related industries, primarily paper and publishing.

Industry and Agriculture

The main industry in New Zealand is stock farming and agriculture. One-third of the country is grazing land and cropland. This land is well-managed, and farming methods are nearly completely mechanized. Therefore, most New Zealand farms are highly productive. As an island nation, New Zealand is isolated geographically. Yet its production methods are so efficient that it can be competitive in the foreign market. Its exports include meat, butter, cheese, and wool, and it ships these products to markets halfway around the world.

Many of New Zealand's farmers have practical experience in electrical and mechanical engineering. They have made their farms so efficient that only 110,000 people work full-time on 70,000 farms and orchards. That comes out to only about 1½ persons working full-time per farm!

New Zealand's mountainous land is good for feeding animals but not for growing crops that must be harvested. That is why New Zealand's 60 million sheep and 9 million cattle are mostly pasture-fed.

The economy depends chiefly on the export of agricultural products. New Zealand ranks first in the world as the exporter of wool, dairy products, and lamb and mutton. Other exports include processed food, textiles, and machinery. New Zealand trades with the U.S., England, Australia, China, and Japan. In recent years, tourism has also become an important industry and source of foreign money.

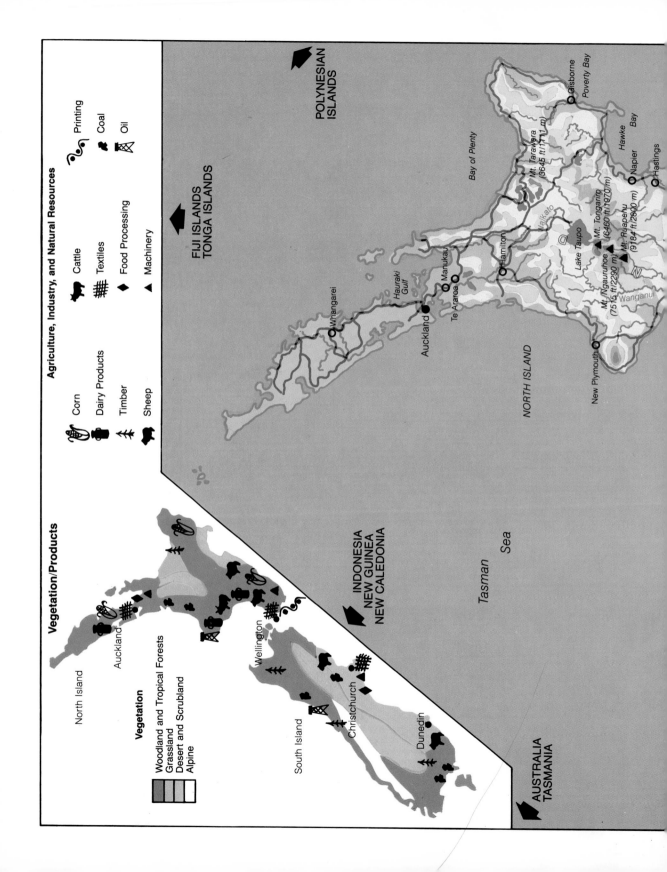

Agriculture, Industry, and Natural Resources

Corn
Dairy Products
Timber
Sheep
Cattle
Textiles
Food Processing
Machinery
Printing
Coal
Oil

POLYNESIAN ISLANDS

FIJI ISLANDS
TONGA ISLANDS

Whangarei
Auckland
Te Aroroa
Manukau
Hamilton
New Plymouth
Wanganui
Lake Taupo
Mt. Tarawera (3645 ft/1111 m)
Mt. Tongariro (6460 ft/1970 m)
Mt. Ngauruhoe (7515 ft/2290 m)
Mt. Ruapehu (9184 ft/2800 m)
Gisborne
Poverty Bay
Hawke Bay
Napier
Hastings
Bay of Plenty
Waikato
Hauraki Gulf

NORTH ISLAND

INDONESIA
NEW GUINEA
NEW CALEDONIA

Tasman Sea

AUSTRALIA
TASMANIA

Vegetation/Products

North Island
Auckland
Wellington
Christchurch
Dunedin
South Island

Vegetation
Woodland and Tropical Forests
Grassland
Desert and Scrubland
Alpine

NEW ZEALAND — Political and Physical

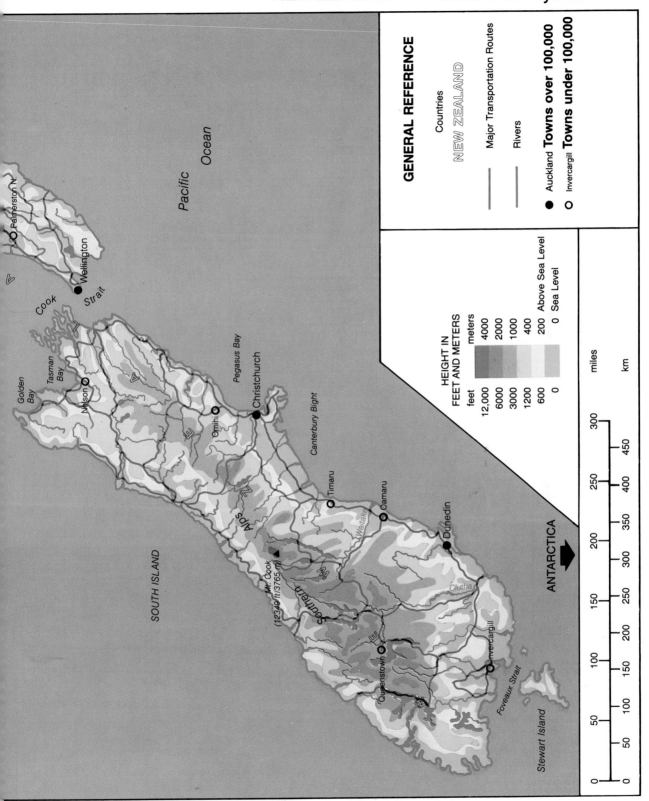

Pacific Ocean

Palmerston N.

Wellington

Cook Strait

Golden Bay

Tasman Bay

Nelson

Pegasus Bay

Christchurch

Omihi

Canterbury Bight

SOUTHERN Alps

Timaru

Oamaru

Waitaki

Dunedin

Clutha r.

Mt. Cook (12349 ft/3765 m)

SOUTH ISLAND

Southern

Queenstown

Invercargill

Foveaux Strait

Stewart Island

ANTARCTICA

GENERAL REFERENCE

Countries

NEW ZEALAND

—— Major Transportation Routes

—— Rivers

● Auckland **Towns over 100,000**

○ Invercargill **Towns under 100,000**

HEIGHT IN
FEET AND METERS

feet	meters
12,000	4000
6000	2000
3000	1000
1200	400
600	200 Above Sea Level
0	0 Sea Level

miles
km

0   50   100   150   200   250   300   miles
0   50 100 150 200 250 300 350 400 450   km

Government

New Zealand is a member of the British Commonwealth. The Parliament is a single-chambered body. Its members are elected every three years. Four seats are reserved for Maori members. Maoris alone vote for these members. The head of the political party which gets more than half of the seats of Parliament becomes prime minister. New Zealand's voting age is 18.

New Zealand is known for its social and civil rights programs and policies. In 1893 it became the first country in the world to allow women to vote. It pioneered programs in benefits for the elderly, as well as labor and management reforms. In addition, it has programs that protect families from money problems caused by sickness, accident, and the death of a breadwinner.

The government looks after children's health needs. For children between the ages of two and thirteen, dental nurses provide regular dental care in school. Children between 13 and 18 receive dental care from private dentists, but the government pays for it. School children in poor health are admitted to health camps.

New Zealand restricts immigration. This is one way it keeps its economy strong. It only accepts certain immigrants. They must be able to fill an occupational need that cannot be filled by people already living there. Also, it does not accept for citizenship people over the age of 45.

New Zealand currency.

Currency

Like those of the United States and Canada, New Zealand's currency is based on a decimal system with dollars and cents. 100 cents = one dollar.

Wellington

Wellington, the capital of New Zealand, is at the southern tip of the North Island. Many North American visitors are surprised at how much it is like San Francisco. Both cities fan out from a large circular harbor. Both are in a basin of steep hills. Cable cars provide public transportation. In Wellington, the houses are built into the sides of the hills, some on stilts. Some homeowners have their own private cable cars. These cars take them from the base of the steep hills to their houses near the top. Wellington residents learn early to climb its steep, narrow streets and sidewalks.

Wellington was settled in 1840. The people who first settled here built their homes across the harbor from where they are today. The fierce winds from the Cook Strait forced them to move their houses on rafts to the present site. Two years after the houses were moved, a fire destroyed them. The settlers rebuilt their homes, this time in clay and brick. When these houses were destroyed by an earthquake, the settlers decided to leave once and for all and resettle in Australia. This plan, too, came to a disastrous end when they were shipwrecked in the harbor. Once more they rebuilt Wellington, this time in wood, and the city survived and has since prospered.

Today Wellington has a population of over 300,000. Besides being the capital of a thriving country, it is home to the National Orchestra and several ballet and opera companies. Its Turnbull Library houses a world famous collection of maps, books, and drawings of the Pacific. Wellington is also the home base for most of New Zealand's major businesses, banks, stock and station agencies, and shipping companies. And, of course, it is the seat of Parliament, which is housed in a building known to New Zealanders as the Beehive, because it looks like one.

New Zealanders in Canada and the U.S.

As a people, New Zealanders enjoy traveling a great deal. Most of them also enjoy coming back to New Zealand. Therefore, very few New Zealanders emigrate to other countries. Most New Zealanders who do emigrate go to Australia or Britain. Australia and New Zealand are both part of the southwest Pacific area known as Australasia. Also, New Zealanders feel stronger cultural ties to Australia and Britain than to North America. In 1984, 14,097 New Zealanders emigrated to Australia and 7812 to Britain. The U.S. came in third with 1842. Following Western Samoa and the Cook Islands (both also in the southwest Pacific), Canada was sixth on the list with 550 New Zealand immigrants.

Wellington, New Zealand's capital city.

Glossary of Useful New Zealand Terms

English is the national language of New Zealand. Much of New Zealand's language is a New Zealand variety of English. Many Maori terms are also a part of the language of New Zealand. Some of these terms are in the list that follows. For an idea of how to pronounce words of Maori origin, see "Language" on page 51.

Aotearoa .... land of the long, white cloud; Maori for New Zealand
aroha .... love and understanding for others
bach or *crib* .... cottage or vacation house
bush .... forest, woods, scrubland
climbing frame .... children's tree house or hut
fizzy .... soda or pop
haka .... traditional Maori war dance, now performed before All Black rugby matches and for ceremonial purposes
kiwi .... the national bird of New Zealand; what people from New Zealand call themselves
mana .... Maori pride or honor
Maoritanga .... the Maori way of doing things
marae .... Maori meeting house or open space around the meeting house
mob .... herd of sheep or cattle
musterer .... cowboy
mustering .... roundup
pa .... Maori community
paddock .... field
pakeha .... foreigner or white person, anyone not Maori
peckish .... hungry
rattle your dags .... hurry up
rousterer .... professional sheep shearer
station .... sheep or cattle ranch or farm
tapa .... clothing made of soft bark
tapu .... taboos or prohibitions
tatou-tatou .... "us-us"; represents goal of Maori-Pakeha unity
tohunga .... village tribal elder
tramping .... hiking
whare .... house

More Books About New Zealand

Listed below are more books about New Zealand. If you are interested in them, check your library. You may find many of them helpful in doing research for some of the "Things to Do" projects that follow.

Isles of the South Pacific. Shadbolt & Ruhen (National Geographic Society)
Kuma Is a Maori Girl. Lawson (Hastings House)
Life on a Lost Continent: A Natural History of New Zealand. Day (Doubleday)

The Maoris of New Zealand. Wiremu (Wayland)
New Zealand: Sunset Travel Guide. (Lane)
New Zealand Yesterday and Today. Mahy (Franklin Watts)
Turi: The Story of a Little Boy. Powell (Longman Paul)
We Live in New Zealand. Ball (Bookwright)

Things to Do — Research Projects

Governments make policies and decisions that can change their countries' alliances and trading partners overnight. During the 1980s, for example, New Zealand developed a policy that bans nuclear arms within its boundaries. This means that nuclear-armed ships will not be allowed into New Zealand ports. This policy affected a major defense treaty New Zealand had had with the U.S. for more than 40 years.

As you read about New Zealand or any country, keep in mind the importance of having current information. Some of the research projects that follow depend on accurate, up-to-date information. This is why current newspapers and magazines are useful sources of information. Two publications your library may have will tell you about recent magazines and newspaper articles on many topics:

The Reader's Guide to Periodical Literature

Children's Magazine Guide

For accurate answers to questions about such topics of current interest as New Zealand's immigration policies, earthquakes, international policies, and trading partners, look up *New Zealand* in these publications. They will lead you to the most up-to-date information you can find.

1. Why is New Zealand earthquake territory? Using your library, find out about the history of earthquakes in New Zealand.

2. New Zealand prohibits nuclear weapons within its boundaries. Check the *Reader's Guide to Periodical Literature* or the *Children's Magazine Guide* to find out how other countries' governments have reacted to New Zealand's position.

3. Learn more about the histories of the Maori and American Indian as their countries were settled by white people. What are the differences in the ways they were treated? What are the similarities? How has this treatment affected their places in their societies today?

4. How far is Christchurch from where you live? Using maps, travel guides, travel agents, or any other resources you know of, find out how you could get there and how long it would take.

5. Write a short report about a resource or industry important to New Zealand's economy. Be sure your information is current, at least within the last year.

6. Imagine that your parents decide to move to New Zealand. Find out more about New Zealand and pick a location. Give your reasons.

7. Imagine you are taking a trip through the North Island of New Zealand. Plan the route. Write an imaginary diary about what you see. Include descriptions of the land, rivers, climate, animals, historical landmarks, and people.

8. See if your library has any books of stories from New Zealand. Find some that you like and read one to a younger friend or brother or sister. Draw a picture to illustrate part of the story.

More Things to Do — Activities

These projects are designed to encourage further thinking and discussion about New Zealand. They offer ideas and suggestions for interesting group or individual projects that you can do at school or at home.

1. Pronounce these names of the seven Maori vessels to discover New Zealand:
    Te Arawa Tainu Matatua Takitimu Aotea Kurahaupo Tokomaru
    The guide for pronouncing Maori words on page 51 will help you.

2. Find the words and music to the Hawaiian Farewell, known to New Zealanders as "Po Atarau." Learn the song and perform it for your friends. What else can you find out about the history of this song?

3. Here is a recipe for a dish served for dessert in New Zealand called Fried Bananas. This will serve four people. You will need:

4 bananas	1 teaspoon (5 ml) cinnamon
¼ cup (62.5 ml) brown sugar	½ cup (125 ml) water
¼ cup (62.5 ml) butter	ice cream

    Lightly fry bananas in half the butter until golden in color. Take them out with a slotted spoon and put in four dishes. Leave the butter in the pan. Add the rest of the butter and the brown sugar and cinnamon. Heat over low heat till the sugar melts. Add the water and cook until the mixture thickens slightly. Put a scoop of ice cream over the bananas in the dishes. Pour the hot sauce over the top.

4. If you would like a pen pal in New Zealand, write to these people:

    International Pen Friends
    P.O. Box 65
    Brooklyn, New York 11229

    Be sure to tell them what country you want your pen pal to be from. Also include your full name and address.

Index